I0439911

SAFETY, SECURITY AND SURVIVAL

IN TODAY'S SOCIAL JUNGLE

by John Tomikel, Phd

ISBN   978 1482746426

I. Surviving in the Urban Environment
a. children
b. financial scams
II. Surviving a Nuclear Disaster
III. Surviving in a Remote Area

final personal notes

FOREWORD

My son, twelve years old at the time, innocently asked me what animal caused the most human deaths. I pondered the question and thought about snakes, bears, lions, tigers, wolves and said bee and wasp stings on land and crocodiles in water. He was pulling my leg and said "People kill more people than any other animal." He was correct of course. Even in the absence of armed conflict people kill each other at a horrendous rate.

Here are some philosophical aspects of survival as well as considerations if you are an innocent person caught up in a combat zone which may be military combat, rioting, or violent protesting. Advice is also given for assault, abduction, home invasions, road rage, and robbery.

If one is living in an area with less than a democratic government then it is a good idea to have a second identity as back-up. Most countries of the world rely on identity papers of some kind. Taiwan has a "life" book that everyone must carry when traveling out of their district. It is an internal passport which has to be renewed periodically and a new photo taken. In the United States our driver's license serves this purpose at the moment. Those who wish to travel by plane and do not have a driver's license must obtain a certified photo identification card. The social security number is another item that is used to keep track of people.

I
Surviving In The Urban Environment

Home Invasion

We lived in a rural setting for the last thirty years and raised two children there. Our nearest neighbor was six hundred feet away. We were apprehensive every time we opened the door at night. We had a plan which included closing the door behind me and opening the door of our mud room. That was our outside entrance and we also had a glass storm door there. If there was some problem with whoever was at the door I could retreat quickly into the house and lock both doors behind me.

Throughout those years many people came to the house at night -ran out of gas – looking for my dog that broke loose – can I use your phone, I hit a deer and my car is disabled. I would send the phone users to a phone hook up in the barn garage and my wife would listen in on their calls. Today, cell phones have all but made land phones obsolete.

The years crept up on me, the children left home, and I felt I was no longer physically able to maintain a rural property and could not adequately protect us from a physical threat. To make matters worse, a young man just down the road had been arrested for multiple burglaries and a young man just up the road was arrested for armed robbery. Both were in and out of prison. We knew them both well but never felt threatened by them. This was a foolish assumption since their behavior was anti-social and probably unpredictable. If someone had asked us about them, we would have assured them that both of these lads were nice kids.

So for security and peace of mind we moved to a condo-house community which had two entrances but no gates. Our complacency was upset at Halloween when pumpkins were smashed about sixty feet into one entrance and two street light posts were knocked over.

It is never wise to ignore safety precautions in this day of overpopulation, unemployment, and poverty. Home is our castle, it is our retreat, but now home invasions have become more frequent. The occurrences of home invasion are statistically low, but these incidents do occur and some consideration must be given to this menace.

We think these events happen to other people who are far from us, but where they occur has certain earmarks that are identifiable. Here is the story of our office secretary Mary.

Mary lived at a rural crossroads with her mother, father, and fourteen year old son. Her husband had died the previous winter. The event occurred when her mother was away for a few days. Mary and her son were in the living room watching television on a warm night in August. A hand crashed through the screen door. The hand held a gun. Mary rushed upstairs, closed the door and dialed the local township police department and gave them quick information.

There were two men wearing ski masks. They

had the father and the son sit on the sofa and asked if there was anyone else in the house beside that lady that ran away. They called for Mary to come down and said they had the family as hostages. Mary's little dog started barking furiously and Mary put the dog in the basement.

Mary's son started giving the bandits some back talk. . Mary told him to keep quiet. Her father also told the boy to not talk.

While the three family members were seated on the couch, one man held a gun on them while the other ransacked the house. Mary told them where she kept her jewelry and money. When they were satisfied they told the family to stay put and not follow them.

Satisfied with their bag of loot the bandits stepped out onto the porch. Mary said she was too stunned to get up and lock the door. The police had waited outside and when the men were away from the door they yelled "police" and fired a shot. One bandit raced back into the house while the police cuffed the other.

The bandit that entered the house said he would take the boy as a hostage. Mary's dad said he would go with him instead. They took off on foot and later came to a car. The grandfather was released and the bandit sped away.

It was just a matter of little time until the police had both bandits in custody. They were both nineteen years old and lived only a few miles from the site of the event.

Mary did not come to work for a week and spent more than a year in therapy. She didn't think she would ever recover from the event.

ACTION

Mary was quick to react to the situation. When an emergency occurs of any type you usually only have about a half minute to make some decisions. You have to make that decision quickly because the future events will muddle your thought processes. In the event of a home invasion you will be quickly incapacitated if you don't respond immediately. You have to consider such a situation and have planned in advance some decisions that you would make.

Do you flee or do you fight, or do you do neither but just accept the situation and try to deal with it? Your reaction would of course depend on the situation and your physical condition, mental condition, age and sex. Your reaction would also depend on the physical environment and the circumstances at the moment. All of these would have to race through your mind in less than a minute.

How have you acted in previous situations? Of course you don't have time to run all of this through your mind as the event plays out, so you have to consider these things as you consider the possibilities of such an event. The fact is you don't know how you will respond to the event until you are involved in it. But, prior consideration will give you an advantage. It's like an acrobat doing a somersault. The acrobat figures out the moves in advance, not while up in the air.

Most parents would risk death to save their family from harm. However, if one of you can get away quickly then do so. Do not let threats of harm to those left behind deter you. If you give up and return to their power then all of you are more at risk since there is no one out there to help you. No, you have to get away and get help. Knowing that someone has escaped their clutches and help is probably on the way should cause the perpetrators to act swiftly and get out of there. The fact that help is on the way would probably protect your loved ones from harm.

Resist with all your effort any attempt to tie you up or put you in the trunk of a car. Try to stay calm and wait for an opening.

Even if you are not physically strong, and there is one intruder, a quick smash in the face and quick flight will get you free. Do not assume you can stay there and fight with the intruder. He has probably picked your place because he has seen there is no one there who is a challenge to him physically. Home intrusions are usually not random acts.

You might react according to your own assessment of the danger involved. You can comply with the request of the intruder and hope he just goes away quickly. However, when an intruder gets compliance he usually stays longer than the time necessary to complete his objective which is usually robbery. Giving him time to linger might increase the chances of molestation. So acts of resistance in word or body language might be an asset in this situation. It might be useful to discuss this type of reaction with family members so that all of you might have some notion as to what the other member is thinking.

In my novel *The Boxer College Murder* there is a scene where the old man of the house feigns illness and old age in order to apprehend the intruder. This is fantasy. The intruder does not care if you have a heart condition or any other illness. He does not have sympathy as a personal attribute.

Have a family plan for escaping the danger. Decide where to run and what to say when you get there. You might have to jump out of a window and receive a minor injury, but that is a small price to pay.

Having a "safe" room in your house is a good idea if you can contact the outside world from there. If you are safe and the intruder says, "If you don't come out I will shoot your father, child, etc. it is probably not a good idea to leave the room, especially if you can contact the outside. Cell phones are a great invention. **It is difficult to get someone to make a decision and choose between alternate disagreeable choices.** If the intruder is capable of killing someone outside the room, then he is capable of killing you when you come out of the room or hiding place. Then you will all be dead and there will be no one left to testify to the event.

Screaming out the window or anytime is a good action. Many assaults have been thwarted by the potential victim screaming and acting as if out of control and disarranged.

An Ounce of Prevention

Develop a home security plan and talk about it with your family and neighbors. You don't have to alarm the neighbors with your paranoia. You can mention it casually and discuss what you would do or they would do under such circumstances and thereby develop a neighborhood plan. Let them know if you have installed alarm systems or any other protective devices.

Have strong bolts and locking devices on your doors. Check the internet for home security tips. Have some system of looking out the door to see who is ringing the door bell. Maybe a wide angle peep hole or a window that looks out on the door. A thick glass storm door is a must. In our old house I could talk to someone outside the door through a window which was handy.

A chain latch is a good security device if you don't have a storm door. It won't stop a determined intruder completely, but it will give you time to escape to a safe room and dial 911 or retrieve your gun.

There are many alarm systems on the market and many plans which contact the police. If these appeal to you then by all means install them. I thought I would install a loud alarm on the side of my house that could be activated by a switch. A ringing alarm would certainly cause an intruder to think twice about lingering. It would alert the neighbors and at least let them know that something wrong was going on.

There was a time when I was in charge of a storage shed for athletic equipment. I had installed a motion sensor since burglary was a possibility. Deer wandering by would set it off and the police were calling me at all hours to come and turn it off. I tried giving them a key to the building, but they did not want to be involved in that manner. I eventually turned the device off and gladly handed the keys over to my successor.

Signs warning possible intruders that the property was protected by alarms tied to the police always seemed like littering to me. However, these signs are effective and a burglar looking at them will probably move on to some other victim.

Of course, you should always be suspicious of someone delivering goods that you have not requested. There are many tricks to get someone to open the door and let a stranger in. Usually it is a pair of strangers. One will engage you in conversation while the other "uses the bathroom."

If an intruder has you under control do not let them transport you anywhere, for instance, to an ATM machine unless you can't possibly avoid it.

Your Burglar Alarm

Most people don't think in terms of burglar alarms, but you probably don't know you have one. If your car keys can activate the illegal entry alarm to your car, you have a burglar alarm. Keep these beside your bed at night and if an intruder enters your home, activate the car alarm and that should get him running. All your neighbors would be looking out the window by then.

This is also a good idea when shopping at the mall. Have your car keys ready when you approach your car. If you should be accosted, then activate the car alarm and if possible throw the keys as far away as you can throw. Over the tops of other cars is a good way to hinder anyone from finding them quickly, even you.

This alarm can be used for many other purposes. For instance, if you are going out to the mailbox on a snowy or slippery day and you should fall and not be able to get up and you have your car keys with you, then you can alert your spouse or neighbor by pressing the alarm. The alarm will sound until your car battery runs out which could be as long as a full day.

Gun in the home

Our rural neighbors always kept a loaded shotgun near the door. When I first went to introduce myself to them the husband greeted me while holding his shotgun. Could the shotgun be effective if an intruder simply broke into the house? Not if its in the front room and he comes in the back door.

We had several loaded hand guns squirreled away in different locations. Fortunately, we never had to use them for protection. My wife kept a loaded handgun in her bed when I was away from home overnight. She had practiced shooting it and was proficient in its use.

If you have a hand gun for protection then you have to be determined to use it. When someone crashes into your home without your invitation then you have to decide what you will do with the gun. Do you just tell them to hold it and you have a gun or do you just blast away? If they are close to you or coming at you then you better blast away.

If the intruder has you covered with his gun then it is not a good idea to go for your gun and try to out-shoot him. You have to play it cool and wait for an opportunity rather than engage in a direct duel.

The **general rules of safety** is avoiding a dangerous situation or location, being aware of your surroundings and that there is possible danger there, and preparedness, to be prepared to act in a situation.

Home Invasion and Legality

Most criminals involved with home invasion are charged with the crimes that they committed in the home rather than with the act of invasion. Connecticut Congressman Chris Murphy proposed in 2008 legislation that would make home invasion a federal crime in the United States.

Home invasion is the act of illegally entering a private and occupied dwelling with violent intent for the purpose of committing a crime against the occupants such as robbery, assault, rape, murder, or kidnapping. Home invasion is generally an unauthorized and forceful entry into a dwelling. In some jurisdictions there is a defined crime of home invasion; in others there is no crime defined as home invasion., but events that accompany the invasion are criminal.

Where home invasion is defined, the definition and punishments vary by jurisdiction. It is not a legally defined federal offense throughout the United States, but is in several states, such as Michigan, Connecticut. Illinois, Florida, New

Hampshire, Louisiana and Las Vegas, Nevada. Legislation of this nature have been introduced in South Carolina and Maryland.

Most countries do not have home invasion laws and the crime is judged from the actions involved in the home rather than the act of invasion.

Home invasion differs from burglary in having a violent intent, specific or general, much the same way as aggravated robbery-personally taking from someone by force-is differentiated from mere larceny (theft alone). As the term becomes more frequently used, particularly by the media, "home invasion" is evolving to identify a particular class of crime that involves multiple perpetrators (two or more); forced entry into a home; occupants who are home at the time of the invasion; use of weapons and physical intimidation; property theft; and victims who are unknown to the perpetrators.

Victims known to the perpetrators is a tricky legal question. Ex-boy friends entering the ex-girlfriends apartment have many offshoots and avenues of defense. The events occurring in those invasions are usually what constitutes criminal activity.

Incidence

Few statistics are available on the crime of home invasion as such, because it is not defined as a crime in its own right in most jurisdictions. Statistics about home invasion found on the Internet are often false or misleading. Persons arrested for what the police or media may refer to as "home invasion" are actually charged with crimes such as robbery, kidnapping, homicide, rape, or assault.

Terminology and home invasion as a crime

The first published use of the term "home invasion" as recorded in the *Oxford English Dictionary* is an article in the Washington Post on 1 February 1912, with an article in the Los Angeles Times on 18 March 1925 clearly indicating the modern meaning of the phrase.

"Home-invasion robberies" were highlighted in June 1995, when the term appeared in the cover story of *The FBI Law Enforcement Bulletin* in an article written by Police Chief James T. Hurley of the Ft. Lauderdale, Florida, area, later republished on the online blog posted by Harvard Business School, Hurley posited that, at the time, the crime could be considered an alternative to bank or convenience store robberies, which were becoming more difficult to carry out due to technological advances in security. In the same article Hurley recommended educating the public about home invasion.

Before the term "home invasion" came in use, the term "hot burglary" was often used in the literature. Early references also use "burglary of occupied homes" and "burglar striking an occupied residence".

Notable examples

One well known home invasion is the November 15, 1959 quadruple murder of the Clutter family by Richard "Dick" Hickock and Perry Edward Smith during a home-invasion robbery in rural Holcomb, Kansas. The murders were detailed in Truman Capote's "nonfiction novel" *In Cold Blood.* However, the perpetrators were convicted of murder, not home invasion.

In another highly publicized incident, two paroled criminals were each charged with three counts of capital murder during a home invasion into a home in Cheshire, Connecticut on July 23, 2007. During the invasion, the mother died of asphyxiation due to strangulation and the two daughters died of smoke inhalation after the suspects set the house on fire. The men were charged with first-degree sexual assault, murder of a kidnapped person, and murder of two or more people at the same time. The state attorney sought the death penalty against the suspects. The first defendant, Steven Hayes, was found guilty of 16 of 17 counts including capital murder on October 5, 2010 and. on November 8, 2010 was sentenced to death. His co-defendant, Joshua Komisarjevsky, was convicted of all 17 counts against him in October, 2011. Both men were sentenced to death. This prompted the state to pass home invasion legislation. It is interesting to note that the time lapse between the crime and the trials was close to three years.

Another home invasion occurred on November 26,

2007 when Washington Redskins star Sean Taylor was murdered during an overnight home invasion of his suburban Miami heme. Four defendants were charged with this crime.

Many U.S. States have what are called "stand your ground" laws. A variation of these is referred to as the Castle Doctrine, in reference to a home being one's castle. These laws protect defending oneself against forcible entry of one's home as part of their definition of justifiable homicide without any obligation to retreat.

As I write this,(Feb. 2013) there was a news article about a man in New Fairfield, Connecticut who shot and killed his fifteen year old son who was wearing a ski mask at night and was out in the yard. Perhaps the publicity given to home invasions get people more apprehensive than they should be. What philosophy can we draw from that tragic incident? What was the fifteen year old doing outside at 1 a.m. and wearing a ski mask?

There is some legal questions concerning where a burglar or potential burglar can be shot without the shooter incurring legal complications. If shot entering the house then the home defense laws kick in. If shot in the backyard, then there might be several questions of legality and complications. However, if you are in the backyard and you tell the perpetrator to stop and he still comes at you, then that is a good defense.

Going Out For The Evening

When I was in my dating days I was surprised one evening when my date announced that she had left a note somewhere saying where she was expecting to go and with whom she expected to be. The note even contained my phone number. I laughed at her caution.

Now I don't laugh anymore since many women and men disappear or are found murdered with no clue as to where they were going or with whom they were going.

If you don't have a friend of confidence that you can tell about your activities then you should leave some sort of note where it can be found by an investigating authority. If you are going on a prolonged clandestine trip then perhaps mail a letter to yourself. When you return you can throw the letter away. If you don't return the authorities will find it.

Police Pull Over

There are too many crimes committed by criminals in "unmarked" police cars to not mention it here. If you are signaled to pull over by what appears to be a police vehicle, marked or unmarked, drive to where there is a group of people or an open store and then pull over. If you have a cell phone and suspect something amiss dial 112 or 9-1-1 and give a report as to what is happening.

One trick a rapist uses is to drive alongside a young woman's car and point toward her tires to get her to pull over. Be aware.

There were eight murders of young women in southwestern Pennsylvania where I was teaching at the time. The sixth victim was at her boy friends house and when she left the house she said she would not stop her car for anyone. She was missing the next day and found murdered. The only conclusion was that someone with a police car pulled her over. There were two more victims after that. A month after the last victim was found the county constable committed suicide. He was a local suspect by his constituents, but there was never any public statements about the coincidences.

Stalking

There are few things more upsetting than someone hanging around you when you do not wish them to be there. There are many psychological reasons for them acting that way, but that is not our concern here. Every state has stalking laws and you should take advantage of them. Once you have initiated the law do not back down and open up for "just a few minutes." Call the police when the stalker is in your protected vicinity. An irritated and frustrated human is capable of almost any violent or mischievous action. The fact that the person continues stalking after the back-off verdict indicates that there is danger to you from even the most harmless looking person.

Definitions and Legal Discussion of Stalking

Stalking is the unwanted or obsessive attention by an individual or group toward another person. Stalking behavior is related to harassment and intimidation and may include following the victim in person or monitoring them by different means, such as hiring a private detective or setting up electronic equipment. The term "stalking" has different meanings in law enforcement, psychology, and psychiatry.

Stalking is also defined as any unwanted contact between two people which directly communicates a threat or places the victim in fear. Legal definitions and intent to resolve difference in definitions and opinion about stalking are still in progress.

Historical references

The term *stalking* has been used in literature since the sixteenth century to refer to a prowler or a poacher. The term *stalker* started to be used by the media in the 20th century to describe people who pester and harass others, initially with specific reference to the harassment of celebrities by strangers who were described as being "obsessed".

One group of authors describe stalking as "a constellation of behaviors in which an individual inflicts upon another individual repeated unwanted intrusions and communications. Stalking can also be defined as the willful and repeated following, watching and harassing of another person. Unlike other crimes, which usually involve one act, stalking is a series of actions that occur over a period of time.

Although stalking is illegal in most areas of the world, some of the actions that can contribute to stalking can be legal, such as gathering information, calling someone on the phone, sending gifts, emailing or instant messaging. They become illegal when they breach the legal definition of harassment e.g. an action such as sending a text is not usually illegal, but is illegal when frequently repeated to an unwilling recipient. In fact, United Kingdom law states the incident only has to happen twice when the stalker should be aware their behavior is unacceptable e.g. two phone calls to a stranger, two unwanted gifts, and following the victim then phoning them.

People characterized as stalkers may be accused of having a mistaken belief that another person loves them, or that they need rescuing. Stalking can sometimes consist of an accumulation of a series of actions which in themselves can be legal, such as calling on the phone, sending gifts, or sending emails.

Stalkers may use threats and violence to frighten their victims. They may also engage in property damage or make physical attacks that are mostly meant to frighten. Less common are sexual assaults, but they do occur.

Many stalkers are former partners and evidence indicates that the mentally ill stalking type of behavior propagated in the media occurs in only a minority of cases of alleged stalking.

Psychological effects on victims

Disruptions in daily life necessary to escape the stalker, including changes in employment, residence and phone numbers, may take a toll on the victim's well-being and lead to a sense of isolation.

Stalking is a form of mental assault, in which the perpetrator repeatedly, unwantedly, and disruptively breaks into the life-world of the victim, with whom they have no relationship, or no longer have. Moreover, the separated acts that make up the intrusion cannot by themselves because the mental abuse, but taken together have a cumulative effect.

According to one study, women often target other women, whereas men generally stalk women only. However, a January 2009 report from the Department of Justice in the United States reports that "Males were as likely to report being stalked by a male as a female offender. 43% of male stalking victims stated that the offender was female, while 41% of male victims stated that the offender was another male. Female victims of stalking were significantly more likely to be stalked by a male (67%) rather than a female (24%) offender."

My Experience

When I was chairman of a department one of the male members dated the secretary of the department. They were both in their early forties. It was a casual date, a one time affair that had some minor sexual activity. Anyway, the man whom I will call Cliff came to me with his tale of romance. It turned out Bernice was happy with the date, but decided to date someone else. Cliff came to me and said things like, "my soul is inside of her and I can't tolerate someone spilling semen all over my soul."

What else could I conclude, except that the man suffered from some sort of hysteria.

Secretary Bernice said that Cliff followed her everywhere. Once when she and her mother went shopping he threw himself over the hood of her car. She backed out quickly and he fell to the street.

This was before the state had stalking laws, but there were other legal channels that Bernice didn't wish to pursue. I thought that Bernice felt she was guilty of encouraging Cliff. I said, one date is not encouragement no matter what transpired on that date.

Bernice changed her phone number. Cliff somehow got the new number.

The situation became so desperate that Bernice asked to be transferred to another department. This still didn't stop Cliff and it seemed to be up to me to do something about it. I consulted the administration and the attitude seemed to be, what do you expect us to do?

I was able to get Cliff an emergency leave with the idea he would live with his sister who lived about two hundred miles away. Cliff liked that idea. But, he didn't go to live with his sister for the six month leave but hung around town and had more time to harass Bernice. I called Cliff on this and arranged a meeting with him in my office. It was on a rainy day. He came into my office and threw his wet umbrella against the wall as he entered.

Eventually, I went to the administration and suggested they set up a medical retirement for Cliff, which they agreed to do, since the events were now getting wide publicity. Part of the agreement was that Cliff would seek medical help in a clinic which was not in our state. That was the last I ever heard of Cliff. He did contact one member of our department and told him he could have all the furniture and wall decorations he had in his apartment. The recipient told me that the decorations consisted of two large paintings, one of a cowboy and the other of a nude woman. The recipient sold the furniture and the paintings and donated the money to a local mental health clinic.

Types of stalkers

Psychologists often group individuals who stalk into two categories: psychotic and non-psychotic.

Stalkers may have psychotic disorders such as delusional disorder or other schizo-type problems.

However, most stalkers are not psychotic, but exhibit disorders such as depression, adjustment disorders or substance dependence. Psychiatrists have a plethora of terms and definitions for many of the varying forms of stalking behavior. Obsessing over a person is part of obsessive compulsive personality behavior. Pursuing another person might be for reasons of anger, hostility, projection, blame, dependency, denial, and jealousy. Many stalkers do not have a feeling toward the pursued, but simply have a longing that cannot be fulfilled due to deficiencies in personality or contradictions between beliefs and society's conventions.

In "A Study of Stalkers" Mullen *et al.*. (2000) identified five types of stalkers:

Rejected stalkers pursue their victims in order to reverse, correct, or avenge a rejection (e.g. divorce, separation, termination).

Resentful stalkers pursue a vendetta because of a sense of grievance against the victims – motivated mainly by the desire to frighten and distress the victim.

Intimacy seekers seek to establish an intimate, loving relationship with their victim. To many of them the victim is a long-sought-after soul mate, and they were 'meant' to be together.

Incompetent suitors, despite poor social or courting skills, have a fixation, or in some cases, a sense of entitlement to an intimate relationship with those who have attracted their amorous interest. Their victims are most often already in a dating relationship with someone else.

Predatory stalkers spy on the victim in order to prepare and plan an attack – often sexual – on the victim.

The 2002 National Victim Association Academy defines an additional form of stalking: The **vengeance/terrorist stalker**. Both the vengeance stalker and terrorist stalker do not, in contrast with some of the aforementioned types of stalkers, seek a personal relationship with their victims but rather force them to emit a certain response favorable to the stalker.

While the vengeance stalker's motive is "to get even" with the other person whom he or she perceives has done some wrong to them (e.g., an employee who believes is fired without justification from the job by a superior), the political stalker intends to accomplish a political agenda, also using threats and intimidation to force his target to refrain from or become involved in some particular activity, regardless of the victim's consent.

Intimacy-seeking stalkers often have delusional disorders involving erotic delusions. With rejected stalkers, the continual clinging to a relationship of an inadequate or dependent person couples with the entitlement of the narcissistic personality, and the persistent jealousy of the paranoid personality. The resentful stalkers demonstrate a feeling or culture of persecution with delusional disorders of the paranoid type of personality.

One of the uncertainties in understanding the origins of stalking is that the concept is now widely understood in terms of specific behaviors which are found to be offensive and, or illegal.

In addition, the personality characteristics that are often discussed as antecedent to stalking may also produce behavior that is not stalking as conventionally defined. Some research suggests there is a spectrum of what might be called "obsessed following behavior." People who complain obsessively and for years, about a perceived wrong or wrong-doer, when no one else can perceive the injury and people who cannot or will not "let go" of a person or a place or an idea comprise a wider group of persons that may be problematic in ways that seem similar to stalking. Some of these people get expelled from their organizations and they may get hospitalized or fired or let go if their behavior is defined in terms of illegal stalking, but many others do good or even excellent work in their organizations and appear to have just one focus of tenacious obsession.

Cyber stalking

Cyber stalking is the use of computers or other electronic technology to facilitate stalking. A booming supply shop industry has sprouted to supply Hi-tech equipment such as computer hacking or monitoring software, hidden cameras, microphones, and even GPS tracking units.

Stalking by groups

According to a U.S. Department of Justice report a significant number of people reporting stalking incidents claim that they had been stalked by more than one person, with 18.2% reporting that they were stalked by two people, 13.1% reporting that they had been stalked by three or more. The report did not break down these cases into numbers of victims who claimed to have been stalked by several people individually, and by people acting in concert. A question asked of respondents reporting three or more stalkers by polling personnel about whether the stalking was related to co-workers, members of a gang, fraternities, sororities, and other organizations did not get an adequate response for reliable conjecture.

Many cases of reported multiple stalking involves family members participating as well as friends of the alpha stalker. Usually the victim has no knowledge of the reason for the harassment.

Delusions of persecution

Publicity about stalking has promoted false claims. One study of 357 claims of stalking found 12 percent to be false. Most of these were made by people suffering from delusions.

My wife and I became acquainted with an author whose paperback novel was made into a major film. He was not able to repeat that success and decided that there was a conspiracy against him. My wife asked, by whom? The answer was vague.

Eventually, he said it was the government and he enlisted Amnesty International to his cause. He claimed that they issued a statement saying he was being treated unfairly by the government. We never saw the statement.

He went so far as to visit Hollywood and made appointments with famous personalities about financing a movie for one of his books. They turned him down. After those interviews he took out a full page ad in the New York Times and detailed how he was prevented from being successful in his enterprises. A full page ad in the New York Times would certainly make one wonder about the mental gymnastics the man was experiencing.

There are, of course, a lot of people who falsify police reports about stalking or being imprisoned by some gang for a brief period of time. Most false reports are for purposes of exploitation or manipulation.

Some groups such as the National Rifle Association and the political Tea Party capitalize on the paranoia of their members and use this to enhance contributions for some cause which may be real or imaginary. These types of groups are dangerous to society since they purport that the government is the enemy of society. We, as voters of course, can change the nature of our government at the ballot box. It is unfortunate that political manipulation of voting boundaries and the influx of big money has corrupted our political system.

Parking Lot Problems

You should, of course, be on your guard when approached by a stranger on a jogging trail or in an isolated parking lot or some other unpopulated area. If the actor has evil intentions then flight is the best response. Even if you are somewhat capable of handling yourself physically you do not know how angry or violent the actor might be. Getting away will assure you that you will not be injured. The old saying, "He who fights and runs away, lives to fight another day" is wisdom.

You should have some intuitive judgment about the danger of the situation. If it is a stranger, assume danger and get out of the area as quickly as you can since attackers are not identifiable by their outward appearance. If you have no chance to run and the actor is out to rob you then give him your money. If the actor wants more than your money then that is another problem to be solved.

In an argument you can always agree with the person and thereby lessen the tension. There is no sense in you getting angry, loosing your temper, and perhaps loosing your composure, which is not a good thing. You don't have to agree with the argument but you are using your words and head to get out of a tight spot. Then hopefully, you can walk away from the situation. By being calm you take away some of the advantage a would-be attacker has. By avoiding saying and doing things that threaten your attacker you take away some of his control. Some form of verbal agreement may disarm the attacker. Physical agreement is another matter and should be resisted with all the courage at one's command.

Reduce Your Risks

Another part of self-defense is doing things that can help you stay safe. Here are some tips from the National Crime Prevention Council and other experts:

Understand your surroundings. Walk or hang out in areas that are open, well lit, and well traveled. Become familiar with the buildings, parking lots, parks, and other places you walk. Pay particular attention to places where someone could hide - such as stairways and bushes.

Avoid shortcuts that take you through isolated areas.

If you're going out at night, **travel in a group**.

Make certain your friends and parents know your daily schedule (classes, sports practice, club meetings, etc.). If you go on a date or with friends for an after-game snack, let someone know where you're going and when you expect to return.

Check out hangouts. Do they look safe? Are you comfortable being there? Ask yourself if the people around you seem to share your views on fun activities - if you think they're being reckless, move on.

Be sure your **body language** shows a sense of confidence. Look like you know where you're going and act alert. Don't slump, hump your shoulders, or hand your head.

When riding on public transportation, sit near the driver and stay awake. Attackers are looking for vulnerable targets.

Carry a cell phone if possible. Make sure it is programmed with the appropriate phone number.

Be willing to report crimes committed and known by you in your neighborhood to the police. Do not assume the crime has nothing to do with you.

Take a Self-Defense Class

The best way - in fact the only way - to prepare yourself to fight off an attacker is to take a self-defense class. Some things you just have to learn in person. A good self-defense class can teach you how to size up a situation and decide what you should do. Self-defense classes can also teach special techniques for breaking an attacker's grasp and other things you can do to get away. For example, attackers usually do not anticipate how their victim might react in ways other than they have conceived - that kick to the groin or jab to the eyes, for instance. A good self-defense class can teach you ways to surprise your attacker and catch him or her off guard.

One of the best things people take away from self-defense classes is self-confidence. The last thing you want to be thinking about during an attack is, "Can I really pull this self-defense tactic off?" It's much easier to take action in an emergency if you've already had some practice sessions. But, remember the first rule and that is to run away from the situation if you can.

A self-defense class should give you a chance to practice your moves. If you take a class with a friend, you can continue practicing on each other to keep the moves fresh in your mind long after the class is over.

Check out your local YMCA, community hospital, or community center for classes. If they don't have them, they may be able to tell you who does.

Scene: You are a woman in an unpopulated parking lot and you approach your car. A man comes out of nowhere and he brandishes a gun. Don't wait for a further explanation or discussion -   start running and screaming. What are your chances of being shot. Actually it is very difficult with a handgun to hit someone who is running, especially at an angle and not directly away. The chances the assailant will actually shoot at you are slim, but don't count on it. If you don't run and you stay with the assailant you are not in a good situation.

If you stay and the actor asks for your keys and for you to get in the car or worse yet the trunk of the car then if you want to survive you must not comply. If the actor has sexual assault in mind then your chances of living after the event are about 50-50. No assailant wants to leave a witness behind who can identify and testify. So your response should be "Take the car, but I am not getting in it." If you have the keys in your possession throw them as far away as you can. At this point the actor may appear violent which is an intimidation ploy. He may even punch you and try to force you into the car. Drop to the ground and cover your head and assume the fetal position. Start screaming. If he tries to pick you up resist with all your strength.

Road Rage

Years ago, before we had children, we had a cabin in the wilds about a hundred miles from our home. We would go there most weekends. It was a late Friday in summer when we decided to use the new four lane highway that led close to our place in the wilds.

Once, when we were about halfway there we were approaching an On-Ramp with a car pulling up to get on. I never thought about it but stayed in the right lane as the car pulled up to a stop. When I passed the car the male driver waved his fist at us. After he got on the road he pulled up alongside of us and continued ranting. Then he pulled very close to the front of our pick up truck and slowed to a crawl. I passed him and my wife gave him the finger. I immediately gave her a diatribe of advice. Sure enough, the guy pulled in front of us and did the same maneuver almost causing a wreck. He slowed down and we passed him again. He did it again, but this time I followed him at the snail pace and when he passed an intersection I drove off and onto a secondary road and made our way to the cabin.

Later, when we had children and they were of driving age I instilled in them that a vehicle was a means of transportation and not an extension of ego or some kind of toy. I believe I succeeded.

People get killed because of road rage. Accidents are caused by road rage. It is best if you consider the other driver as an idiot and avoid confrontation with crazies. We all make minor mistakes in driving, like pulling out in front of another vehicle, stopping abruptly, or driving at a speed out of sync with other drivers. However, it is best not to confront other drivers since you don't know their mental frame of mind or if they are carrying fire arms. Don't stop to explain to the other driver why you pulled out in front of him.

The following are common manifestations of road rage:
Generally aggressive driving, including sudden acceleration, braking, and close tailgating.

Cutting others off in a lane, or deliberately preventing someone from merging.

Chasing other motorists.

Flashing lights excessively.

Yelling or exhibiting disruptive behavior at roadside establishments.

Driving at high speeds in the median of a highway to terrify drivers in both lanes.

Rude gestures such as the finger.

Shouting verbal abuses or threats.

Intentionally causing a collision between vehicles.

Hitting other vehicles.

Assaulting other motorists, their passengers, cyclists or pedestrians

Exiting the car to attempt to start confrontations, including striking other vehicles with an object.

Threatening to use or using a firearm or other deadly weapon.

Throwing projectiles from a moving vehicle with the intent of damaging other vehicles.

You might like a good fight or a good argument, but it is better to exit the scene. The other person has no meaning to you or your life so why bother with him or her. There was a situation in North Carolina where two soccer moms where in a confrontation at a stop sign. The one in the car behind got out, moved up to the front car and shot the other mom. When brought to the police station she kept saying, "I don't believe I did that, I just don't believe I did that." I was never able to find or hear the outcome of that case.

Instant Situations

There was an outdoor equipment show and I had signed up for a booth to sell books, such as this one. I hired a local lad to help run my booth so that I did not have to be there the full fourteen hours of the day. It was a week long affair.

When there was a lull in the activity I would wander around and see what other merchandise was for sale and looked at the exhibits. There were also programs and contests in progress throughout the days of the show.

I always considered myself to be a warm friendly fellow and feed back assured me that I was. Like most humans I am ready for conversation and communion with my fellow humans.

There was a knife vendor at the show and I visited his booth. As I looked at his display cases a large fellow moved up to the booth. I said to the vendor, "Here's a customer, sell him a knife."

The large fellow looked at me and said, "If he sells me a knife, I will cut your throat."

Whoa. What response could I give to that, if there should be a response. The guy was staring at me.

The vendor said, "I hope you fellows know each other."

I said, "No, I never saw this man before in my life. I guess you better not sell him a knife." Then I walked away.

I was tempted to be smart-ass and say something like, "The home should be more stringent with their overnight passes." That would not have been a good idea. Confrontation is never the best policy in an unknown situation.

I have a permit to carry a gun and I did have it in my back pocket at the time. I am not certain what I would have done, but if it appeared I was in danger of bodily harm I am certain I would have used it.

Often, some remark or action can be taken as an act of hostility. The best response is to excuse yourself from the situation as quickly as possible.

There is no need to challenge someone or to give a hostile response, especially to a stranger who has no meaning in your life. Agreeing with the person is often a good way to tone-down a tense situation.

ATM -Automatic Teller Machines are convenient, but they have often been the scene of robberies after money has been withdrawn. Keep this in mind as you go to the machine. If you hae a choice, visit the machine in daylight, rather than darkness.

A Life Lesson

There was an incident in my life that I think about frequently which has nothing to do with survival, but it is a good life lesson. I was at a restaurant up in the hills and ordered an Italian sausage sandwich. When the long bun sandwich was put in front of me I pulled it open and found the cut of sausage was a little over an inch in length and the rest was made up in sauce. I was all set to chew out the waitress so she could pass my protest on to the cook or boss.

When the waitress arrived I opened the roll, showed it to her and said, "look at this and for that high price." She looked at me with compassion and said, "I know, isn't that terrible."

She had immediately deflated the situation and gave me the impression she was "on my side."

I often think about that situation and how she skillfully pulled the rug out from under me.

A Bad Situation

We built a home on the outskirts of a small town of ten thousand souls. A banker's wife, Sally, had disappeared on a Friday evening and a ransom request was delivered to the husband who immediately contacted the police. The FBI was called in. A farmer checking his newly planted orchard found Sally's body.

It was only a matter of two weeks when the culprit David was apprehended and brought to trial. He had a lot of witnesses ready to testify that he was in town all day Saturday and Sunday. However, an insect specialist testified that Sally was killed sometime Friday evening because of the life cycle of insect egg to larva that involves insects laying eggs in dead animals or humans.

David had lured Sally into his vehicle parked in an empty church lot by saying that the community was going to honor her husband and the intentions were to be kept secret until the plans had been worked out. The police found the entire scenario on David's computer. He had tape, handcuffs, binding cord etc. listed there. He did not realize that erased material is still on the computer somewhere and a computer hack could get it surfaced. When the police arrested David they took his computer as well as arms and plenty of ammunition. David received the death penalty and it has been almost twenty-five years since the sentence. The penalty seems to be "death by old-age."

Late Note: David died in prison just after I wrote this. The coroner said, "Of natural causes."

I often replay the scene and wondered what Sally's reaction should have been when David pulled a gun on her and started to immobilize her, probably saying he meant her no harm. If she had the foresight and not been taken by surprise she might have fought him and if he did have a gun and used it the car would have had blood in it and this is almost impossible to remove without burning the vehicle. She might have reasoned that if she was going to die she at least could leave this bit of evidence for the police to find.

If a gunman says he is not going to harm you but wants you to get in the trunk of his or your car or riding with him then let him prove it by refusing to go along with his request. Again, I repeat, it is difficult to get people to make a decision when all the possibilities are disagreeable. The decision here is to flee and if flight is impossible to resist with all the strength within you and screaming as loud as possible.

If a kidnapper says he is willing to shoot you while in the parking lot, just imagine how his incentive would increase once he gets you alone in an isolated area. **No, don't go.** it would be best to get shot in a parking lot than in some isolated wilderness. You cannot appease someone who has a murderous intent. The odds of an abductor shooting you in a parking lot are in your favor, something like 8 to 1, but you have to have courage in this situation.

Tivadar Soros on surviving official terror

Tivadar Soros was a Jew living in Budapest when the Hungarian government collapsed and a pro-Nazi government took over the country. In his book *Masquerade* he explains his survival techniques. Jews were being murdered on the street as well as being rounded up and sent to the infamous death camps. Soros anticipated the events and had obtained false and forged documents giving him a different identity, a Christian identity. There were even documents that certified a Christian circumcised for medical reasons. He obtained these for his sons. He obtained false documents for each family member and separated them into different sections of the city. It was best for survival if they didn't stick together. They would meet occasionally and compare notes.

"Life requires balancing internal feelings and instincts against external requirements and needs." He had to constantly remind his proud mother-in-law that some humility was necessary to survival. There was also some uncomfortable conditions that had to be endured. Survival was the ultimate goal.

In the screen play *I Claudius* the Emperor Claudius tells his son that the next emperor will be Nero and he Claudius has made arrangements for his son to live in England. The son said he will not be a coward, he is a Roman, and will defend himself in Rome. Claudius says in a calm manner, "Then you will be dead before the end of that day."

When the ghetto was established, Soros advised people not to go there to live. In the ghetto they would easily be rounded up and massacred. He believed that the best chance of survival was to go underground. In his own case, he was able to get forged papers and obtain a new identity.

The Germans had set up a Jewish Council as a coordinating body. They would tell the council how many workers were needed and where they should gather. Soros believed the council was detrimental to the survival of Jews. His advice was if you are called to meet at a certain place then don't go and go underground. You might get caught, but you are going to die anyway so why not take your chances on the outside. If you are in the inside you are already doomed.

"The citizen should not accept injustice or arbitrariness from the state to which he belongs. If his life is endangered by an unjust action by the state, he is morally justified in fighting back."

"In times of danger the biggest problem is getting people to choose among unpleasant options."

Soros reiterates the Hungarian proverb "A liar must have a good memory." In other words remember your story if you have to repeat it and don't want contradictions.

"Courage is an intangible quality that you either have or you don't have. If a coward tries to act like a hero something is bound to go wrong."

"Most people do not achieve success in

proportion to their capacities. Favorable circumstances plays a vital role...it's unfortunate when a person who is merely lucky mistakes his success for wisdom."

"Nothing works better against terrorists than terror."

A man thought he had friends in high places, but he was sent off to the camp. "This man valued his good connections more than his life."
"It is remarkable how people always exploit the weak, the unprotected, the uneducated."

Believing you have friends in high places and relying on them is a sure road to disaster. If you want to survive, the rule is to trust no one completely.

Turf Rules

Some years ago I was with a group who would stay overnight in London, England. My room mate Bob and I went out to take in the town. We didn't know exactly where we were, but engaged in some open market buying from a vendor at a table who claimed to be an immigrant from Sicily. He was small, determined and physically fit. Bob was a head taller and at least fifty pounds heavier. We were obviously cheated in the exchange rate. I pointed this out to Bob and he started pounding on the table and threatening the vendor. Other vendors of similar build and complexion were quickly interested in our drama.

Our vendor started spitting on the ground and saying things like, "America, Viet Nam" which was a hot topic at that time. I pulled Bob away and walked with him down the alley and explained, no matter how tough he was, we were on their turf. Bob may have gotten a piece of the guy, but he would have fared much worse; we would have fared much worse. In any conflict, the resident has an advantage over a stranger.

RIOTS AND RIOTING

A **riot** is a form of civil disorder characterized often by disorganized groups lashing out in a sudden and intense rash of violence against authority, property, or people. While individuals may attempt to lead or control a riot, riots are typically chaotic and exhibit **herd behavio**r, and are usually generated by civil unrest.

Riots often occur in reaction to a perceived grievance. Historically, riots have occurred due to poor working or living conditions, government, oppression, taxation, or conscription. conflicts between ethnic groups, food supply or religions. the outcome of a sporting event or frustration with legal channels through which to air grievances.

Riots typically involve vandalism and the destruction of private and public property. The specific property to be targeted varies depending on the cause of the riot and the inclinations of those involved. Targets can include people, shops, cars, restaurants, state-owned institutions, and religious buildings.

Some rioters have become quite sophisticated at understanding and withstanding the tactics used by police in such situations. Manuals for successful rioting are available on the internet.

Dealing with riots is often a difficult task for police departments, and police officers sent to deal with riots are usually armed with shields and guns designed for riots. Police may also use tear gas, water hoses, attack dogs, and stun guns to stop rioters.

Riots Dangerous to the Innocent Bystander

Urban riots are riots in the context of urban decay, provoked by conditions such as discrimination, poverty, high unemployment, poor schools, poor healthcare, housing inadequacy and police brutality and bias. Urban riots are closely associated with race riots and police riots.

Sports riots can be sparked by the losing or winning of a specific team. Fans of the two teams may also fight. They are generally seen in two sports, soccer and ice hockey. Players rarely join in such riots, which usually occur in and around the playing field or in the streets or stands. Side note: There was a melee at a baseball game in Pittsburgh where people in the crowd just started a brawl, punching each other. A colleague of mine had attended the game. He said he was sorry that he was away from the action since he would have liked to participate in the event and get to punch out people. I couldn't believe what I was hearing.

In a **race riot** the key factors are race or ethnicity. Usually these are started by some unfounded rumor and the minority race or ethnic group becomes the target. Neighborhoods may be invaded and there is widespread destruction and unfortunately loss of life.

In a **religious riot** the key factor is religious membership. The rioting mob targets people and properties of a specific religion, or those believed to belong to that religion. Mistakes of religious identity are often made and anyone caught up in these is in a precarious position.

Religious minorities in a predominantly Muslim culture have been systematically terrorized and, it seems, encouraged by the governments. Even those Muslims who differ from the majority sect have been terrorized and continue to be so. Any outsider caught up in these inter-religious wars is in double jeopardy.

It is almost mind blowing to read about some American arrested by Iranian police as they were hiking through the mountains of the country. Why would a sane person go into a hostile territory for some recreation that could be had in another place?

It is certainly a good idea to know the laws of a country when you are going to visit it. At least the laws pertaining to your way of life should be examined. For instance, if a woman agrees to go to a man's apartment in Italy she cannot bring about the charge of rape. If a woman goes to a man's apartment then sex is an assumption of both parties. Similarly, the penalty for selling drugs in Singapore is death. In many Islam dominated countries a thief is punished by removal of his hand.

It was a long time ago when we planned to travel to Taiwan and had all the formalities covered. At the last moment President Carter recognized the communist leadership of mainland China as the legitimate rulers of China. The state department said they could not guarantee our safety. We were to travel with friends from Taiwan and so we counted on their influence to protect us.

There were several incidents where we were accosted and suffered some tense moments. The Lion's Club of Taiwan gave us a small lapel flag to wear and this gave us some protection. Our fair skin was an obvious indicator that we were not Taiwanese. Some Americans we met later were wearing a Canada flag on their lapels. In fact, one friend of mine who is a world traveler, always carries a metal Canada flag with him wherever he goes.

Another thing happened on that Taiwan trip. We were given shots for Cholera. The shot wiped me out and my voice couldn't be heard above a whisper. It took almost a week before the voice returned to normal. We should have obtained the injection at least ten days before we departed.

Some Riot Incidents

The term Watts Riots of 1965 refers to a large-scale riot which lasted 6 days in the Watts neighborhood of Los Angeles California in August 1965. By the time the riot subsided, 34 people had been killed, 1,032 injured, and 3,438 arrested. The cause of the riot is believed to be a reaction to the record of police brutality and racial injustices suffered by black Americans.

Los Angeles Riot of 1992 : Rodney King, a black parolee, was involved in a high speed car chase that ended with Rodney being beaten by four white policeman. The four policemen were brought to trial and acquitted of all charges of unnecessary force. People of the predominantly black and Hispanic neighborhood gathered in the street. Burning and looting began slowly and then intensified over four days, with the result of 53 deaths and thousands of injuries.   An interesting note is that more than half of the people arrested were Hispanic.

An event in the L A Riot of 1992

At approximately 6:45 pm, Reginald Oliver Denny, a white truck driver who stopped at a traffic light at an intersection was dragged from his vehicle and severely beaten by a mob of local black residents as news helicopters hovered above, recording every blow, including a concrete fragment connecting with Denny's temple and a cinder block thrown at his head as he lay unconscious in the street.

The police never appeared, having been ordered to withdraw for their own safety. One of his attackers, Damian Williams, was sent to prison. At the time, Denny was rescued by an unarmed, African American civilian named Bobby Green Jr. who, seeing the assault live on television, rushed to the scene and drove Denny to the hospital using the victim's own truck, which carried twenty-seven tons of sand.

Denny had to undergo years of rehabilitative therapy, and his speech and ability to walk were permanently damaged. Although several other motorists were brutally beaten by the same mob, Denny remains the best-known victim of the riots because of the live television coverage.

At the same intersection, just minutes after Denny was rescued, another beating was captured on video tape. Fidel Lopez, a self-employed construction worker and Guatemalan immigrant, was ripped from his truck and robbed of nearly $2,000. Damian Williams, mentioned previously, smashed his forehead open with a car stereo as another rioter attempted to slice his ear off. After Lopez lost consciousness, the crowd spray painted his chest, torso and genitals. Rev. Bennie Newton, an African-American minister who ran an inner-city ministry for troubled youth, prevented others from beating Lopez by placing himself between Lopez and his attackers and shouting "Kill him and you have to kill me, too". He was also instrumental in helping Lopez get medical aid by taking him to the hospital.

Lopez survived the attack, undergoing extensive surgery to reattach his partially severed ear, and months of recovery.

Surviving a Riot

We are talking "Survival" here and assuming you are not a part of those rioting. Of course, the obvious response if rioting is taking place or about to take place is to get out of the area as quickly as possible and then watch the late night news on television.

If you are in a vehicle and the vehicle is caught in a traffic blockage then lock the doors and stay in the vehicle. If it appears the traffic is permanently immobilized then you might want to leave it and proceed on foot. You can go to a residence and ask for asylum until the rioting has died down. Most people will help someone in need.

If looting, arson, and smashing windows are occurring then going into a store or business would not be a good option.

You might have a handgun or other weapon in your vehicle and these should be brandished as a last resort. If someone sees the weapon and still insists on attacking you then don't hesitate to use it. This is a survival situation. Your life is worth much more than the attacker's.

Unfortunately humans have what I call the "cat response" which is curiosity. We want to hang around and watch the drama unfold. Because you are not participating in the riot does not mean that you won't be dragged into it by the rioters or the authorities who hopefully have arrived by now and are dealing with the situation. The video you take might make the evening news, but you won't be around to see it if you are dead. Get out of there.

Children

We were visiting Niagara on the Lake Canada and were in a restaurant ready to dine when our twelve year old son and eight year old grandson came to join us. My son had a serious expression and said "we didn't tell him anything." Upon further questioning the boy said some man started asking him questions and they just ran away from him.

It was only a matter of minutes when a well-dressed man came to our table and apologized. He said he asked the boys if they were on vacation and visiting Canada. I assured him everything was in order and thanked him for coming to me and said words to the effect that "It is unfortunate we can't be friendly to children anymore without raising some suspicion."

Pass Word: You develop a secret password between you and your child and the child should not share the password with anyone, not even siblings.   If Uncle Leon stops to pick the child up after school he must give the child the password before that child gets in the car with him. If he doesn't give the password then the child goes back into the school and consults the teacher.

When my daughter was in second grade there were a lot of stories on TV about alien abductions and it was at the height of one of the UFO crazes. She would not enter the car with me unless I gave her the password since she feared I might have been abducted and replaced with an alien. That may have seemed farfetched, but I appreciated her caution.

Adults can share passwords also. My wife and I had some keywords for situations that would steer the conversation or the action in another direction. For instance, when she used the word "pearl" it meant I was starting to engage in a topic that was treading on forbidden ground. Other words were used to indicate we should "get out of here" as soon as possible.

If you are in a high risk business or carry a lot of money, it might be prudent to have a signal that you are in a dangerous situation when you make the phone call to home. Another signal might mean to contact the police immediately with a description of you and your car. Perhaps this is paranoid and upsetting, but it only takes a couple of words, "just in case." The words should be those that you don't used often but can be worked into a conversation.

Abductions of children are a rare event and when they do occur they make national and international headlines. Somehow you have to let your children know these things do occur without spooking them. You might tell this true story at an appropriate time. "This little girl was coming home from school and this man jumped out of his car and grabbed her and was going to put her in his car. The little girl started kicking and screaming and this attracted some neighbors. The man got scared and put the girl down and got in his car and drove away. The police arrested him because they had a description of the car the man was driving."

Needless to say, teenagers and school students should absolutely inform parents where they are going and with whom, when they will be leaving and when they expect to return.

An acquaintance of mine had a sixteen year old daughter that didn't obey his curfew of ten o'clock on school nights and midnight on Saturday. Eventually it got down to where he made the threat that if she didn't obey the rules she had to leave the house. She decided to leave the house and move away. He said it really hurt to see her waiting at the street corner to catch the bus with one suitcase at her side. Later, he confided, he found out where she was living with a distant relative and would slip money to her. She did finish high school with a GED and did go on to college.

FINANCIAL CONSIDERATIONS

Strong Arm Tactics

Back in the good-old days there used to be a set of hoodlums who would go up to store owners and tell them to make payments or something bad would happen to them or their store. This situation still exists in some parts of the world, but hopefully not in our country.

Something seems to have taken the place of these intimidation events. Con artists and scammers have begun to use similar tactics with consumers, especially those over 50 who don't have the stamina to resist very well. Fear and intimidation can go a long way, especially if the terror is increased if one should go to the police.

If you have missed a loan payment you may become victim to this intimidation. You're told to pay to avoid a bogus court summons, or you're told a virus will ruin your computer unless you pay a fee. It is possible someone might even come to your home, especially if they note your age and consider your vulnerability.

There have been instances that people were told a contract was put on their life. In order to avoid death a payoff is necessary. The FBI recorded 1,324 such instances in the year 2012. We can only imagine how many people paid up without contacting the police or the FBI. The criminals often use Facebook and other online sites to get personal information about you and your family to make the threats seem real. You have to limit the amount of information you post online.

There was a collection agency in my town of Erie that set up a sham court complete with robed judges and bailiffs. People went to this courtroom and believed they were in a legal jurisdiction. Eventually the collection company was put out of business.

Scammers may claim to be from social security, Medicare, Medicaid, local courts – anything to get information on you and then use this information to get money from you.

In these hard times it is possible to miss a utility payment. Even if you haven't missed one a scammer might convince you that your utility was about to be shut off if you don't make an additional payment of an assessment. If you have caller ID, they can often make the ID appear to be the company they claim to be representing.

Most utilities will send you at least two notices before they take action against you. If someone comes to your door saying they represent the utility company, don't let them in. Call the company or maybe the police.

In any instance, before you pay out anything, confirm the debt with the company. There is legislation pending in congress to expand fraud education for older people and improve complaint reporting, as well as federal monitoring.

Last year I was browsing on the computer when an interesting article caught my eye. I had trouble calling it up and when I did get it my computer froze and an FBI message appeared saying I had violated computer use code #33425-89 NS. It was a very official looking document. I had to pay a fine of three hundred dollars to get my computer released for operation. There were instructions given on how to pay the fine. I had to get a payment card from some source and send the payment with that card.

Fortunately, my son was home from college at the time and he assured me it was a scam and he would fix the situation. He worked on it a couple of hours and then finally reset the computer to the settings it had a day before the scam appeared on my screen. This sent my computer back to the original settings at the time of purchase.

Financial Security

Everyone knows that we should spend less money in a month than we take in. But there are two philosophies on this situation. If we save and put away for a rainy day while we are young, then we will have something of financial contentment in our older years. The antithesis of this is "why not get the things I want while I am young and have red blood to enjoy them, and then pay for these in my later years when I will not be as active. Thus, we go into debt and hope to pay off that debt as the years go by. We may think "Social Security" will help us pay for the flings we had in youth, but studies point out that Social Security should be an accompaniment to other forms of retirement income.

Unsolicited Calls

One of the first rules of safety is to hang up on unsolicited offers. Don't ask for sales information from cold callers. They could claim you offered to purchase what they were selling.

Free equipment. That is, it will be free to you because Medicare or Medicaid will pay for it. Medicare and Medicaid and most insurance companies don't pay for most equipment. When they do, most often a doctor's recommendation or written prescription is required.

You will know this situation in advance because you have talked to a physician beforehand.

Robocalls are obvious recorded calls that you can easily detect. They are illegal unless you have contacted the company. Assume any prerecorded sales pitch is the work of scammers.

If you object to a caller and he says "give me your phone number, and your name and number will be deleted from this file, don't give him your number. An automatic device call does not give the operator your phone number. This scam alerts callers to a working number.

Do not pay for anything you did not order. Some scammers will send you merchandise and a bill for it. The bill usually comes after the merchandise is delivered and accepted into your home. Do not even agree to send the merchandise back. Ignore all contact from the senders.

The following is interesting and deserves some thought. I was sent a four page questionnaire about hearing aids. My answers would be strictly confidential and recorded by an independent consultant. In return for my cooperation the hearing aid company would send me a packet of free batteries for my hearing aid. Just put down my name and address and check the battery packet number I wish to have sent. This is not world-shaking, but it does give the hearing aid company an assurance that I do have a hearing aid. There does not seem to be evil intent here, but it is an interesting sidelight on marketing to me.

Property Repairs

Old people are not the only ones susceptible to scams. I mentioned my cabin in the wild somewhere else in this work. The cabin had been in existence for a couple of years when a pick-up truck with three men in it stopped in the driveway. It seems they had just returned from a job of putting liquid tar on a driveway and had a half tank of liquid tar left. They would put the left over tar on my tar paper roof for $14, just to get rid of it. That seemed like a good deal.

The trio consisted of a hefty man about thirty years old, a thinner man about the same age and an older man around sixty. The thin man was on the roof while the hefty man ran the pump mechanism to the hose. The older man kept circling behind me. This got me worried. The cabin was in an isolated area about two hundred feet off the road. They were speaking a foreign language to each other and after thinking about it I decided they were Roma.

After about fifteen minutes I said I would get the money from my truck. When I counted it out I only had eleven dollars and told the hefty man I would give him a check for the three dollars. He said, "Wait, there is some mistake, it is $14 a gallon and we have already used at least three gallons."

Since, I obviously didn't have any more money on me the hefty man said he would accept the eleven dollars if I didn't contact the police or give him bad references. They drove off with my eleven dollars and when I went to check the roof there was a hole in the tar paper where the thin man obviously had slipped and torn the paper.

When I discussed this with a colleague he said I got off cheap for eleven dollars. The police said they knew the con men were working in the area, but they were gone by the time they had a chance to confront them.

Today, a cell phone would eliminate some of that problem. I could call my wife and describe the situation as well as the vehicle and the participants. My wellbeing could have been in danger.

The most common scams for property owners involve problems with roofs, water drainage, chimneys, driveways, fences, and plumbing. Of course, get references if you can and follow up on these. If not, deal with someone who advertises continuously in your local newspaper. By all means get a quote estimate on the project in writing.

My daughter hired a consultant to look at her chimney. She told the man whatever he recommended to be done would be done by another contractor. Therefore, he would not have the tendency to recommend unnecessary work. This isn't always foolproof, but it is a consideration.

Once you know what work has to be done, you can get two or more estimates on the cost of the project.

When we moved into our new house, we still had contact with the handyman who worked on the old house. He has been willing to do any work we need done on the new house even though he travels a greater distance to get here.

Inheritance Scams

When someone you never heard of leaves you a lot of money you can be certain it is a scam. Often, in order to collect the inheritance you have to pay a fee to have it run through the legal system. Don't do it.

I was once informed of such an inheritance from an actual "relative" in Europe. Nobody in my family of European relatives ever had much money so I told the go-between to take his fee out of my inheritance. He said he needed an advance to free the money from bank litigation. I asked if he could send me some written material concerning this situation, since I am had of hearing. He never contacted me again.

You are notified that you have been involved in a group consumer legal lawsuit and you and the other plaintiffs have won the suit and now you are entitled to a settlement. This may be true, but there are never any legitimate fees that you have to pay to claim your money.

We did receive some money from a class action lawsuit because we had taken a trip to Europe and used our credit cards. The lawsuit involved the exchange rate with foreign currency at the time we were in Europe. The total income was less than twenty dollars on each of our credit cards. We did not have to contact anyone and the money was sent to us automatically at the conclusion of the settlement. Lawyers probably made a bundle on that one. They probably earned it.

You cannot win a lottery when you have never bought a ticket for it. No one will buy you a lottery ticket without your knowledge. You are not automatically given a lottery ticket because you made a deposit in a bank, or purchased some furniture, or other such activity. If someone has purchased a lottery ticket for you as a gift then you should have it in your possession.

Kindly old Grandma

It is almost unbelievable that people are taken in by this scam. A lady in my home city was contacted by a "bail bondsman" in Canada. It seems her grandson had a run-in with the law and needed money to buy his way out. She even spoke to her grandson for a minute but he was in a confined area and the voice was somewhat garbled. He called her by name. He could only talk to her for a minute and had to hand the phone back through the bars. The method of money transfer was through wiring it via Western Union to the bail bondsman in Canada. She was alerted by a bank teller who "didn't want to pry" but was curious. An effort to catch the culprit did not meet with success.

It took two days for all the transactions and by the time the woman realized she had been conned she was out over forty thousand dollars. She didn't bother to call her grandson's cell phone number. He was living alone in Nevada and going to his job every day.

Perhaps in this situation a code word might have been handy. Even without a code word there should have been a red flag waving.

My friend Jerry got such a call from an officer representing his son who had been arrested for a traffic violation across the border in another state. The arresting officer asked Jerry if he would drive the sixty miles and pay the boy's fine. Jerry told the officer he wouldn't do it. His son had really been arrested and arrived safely home the following day, having spent the night in jail. I wish I had Jerry's fortitude and sensibility.

The Nigerian Ploy

By now, the Nigerian Ploy is well known, but there are still people sucked into it every year. It goes something like this. There is a man connected with the Nigerian government who wishes to establish accounts in the United States, but he doesn't know anyone here. He has fourteen million dollars in the account and will give you five percent of it if you agree to be his contact in the United States. You agree and receive some legal looking papers. One hitch, the account needs about four to ten thousand dollars to be freed in order to be sent to the United States. Need I say more?

In the early days of this scam, one man who took the bait actually went to Nigeria to "iron things out." He had packed two suitcases. At the customs entrance he was charged one thousand dollars for each suitcase he was bringing into the country. He was unable to find his contact in Nigeria.

Offshoot of the Nigerian Ploy

You receive a notice that you could be a distributor of
funds for some insurance or other company. If you
agree, they will send you the money for distribution
and you will deposit this money in your checking
account and write checks from your checking account
and send them to those people on the list, usually
three people with P.O. addresses. You receive a check
for ten thousand dollars and you have three names
and addresses to distribute funds to. The funds to be
distributed are not even numbers such as two
thousand dollars. They are numbers such as $1973.18.
You must not delay and send these funds immediately.
So you do it before the bogus ten thousand dollar
check you received has cleared your bank. This is a
legally difficult situation, but some states now have
laws covering such scams.

A London Story

I was in London England, absolutely dead broke and
wandering the streets and waiting for my plane ride
back to the States when I came across an interesting
situation. My credit card had been canceled for some
glitch that I learned later was a protective device by
the credit card company.

There was a betting game going on. One man
had a small portable table and had three cards on it,
two jacks and a king. He would shuffle the cards,
place them face down, and you could place a bet and

pick out the king, if you could. The man placing bets was obviously drunk and losing money on each shuffle.

The third man who appeared to be an observer said to me "The dealer is cheating the man." It was obvious, of course. Then the third man said he was going to get some of that money and started placing bets. The drunken man would pay the dealer and the dealer would give the third man his payment.
The third man asked me to put my finger on a card so the dealer couldn't change it while he fished out five quid. The dealer said that was okay with him. I put my finger on the card.

Finally, the dealer said all bets would be five quid. The shuffle was made and it seemed obvious which card was the king. The third man said to me, "Tell him you had five quid on that card."

The dealer looked at me and asked, "Did you have five quid on the card?"

I really needed the money since my plane departure was near midnight, but I said, "No."

The men played out the game. The drunk said he was broke and showed an empty wallet. The dealer folded up the table and walked away. I was upset that I didn't say "yes" and could have enjoyed a fine dinner.

It took about a month for the realization to set in. How could I have been so stupid? The entire episode was created to con me out of money. The card in question had never been turned over and I assume it was not the king and I would have been out five quid. I don't know what I would have done since I had no money. I probably would have given the dealer my wrist watch or looked for a copper. I did understand pounds and pence, the English currency of that day. To this day, I have no idea about the value of five quid.

II. SURVIVING A NUCLEAR DISASTER

All nuclear explosions cause light, heat, and a blast of air. These occur immediately. Explosions also create large quantities of dangerous radioactive fallout particles, most of which fall to earth during the first 24 hours after the blast.

People closest to the explosion would probably be killed. Those a few miles away would survive but be in immediate danger from heat, fires, and the wind storm.

When a nuclear explosion occurs, great quantities of pulverized earth and dust are sucked up into the atmosphere forming the characteristic mushroom cloud. Radioactive gases produced by the explosion condense and become part of the debris. In a short time these particles fall back to earth. The particles then give off radiation mostly in the form of invisible gamma rays. Therefore, the first few hours after the explosion are the most dangerous period. Areas close to the nuclear explosion might receive fallout within 15 to 30 minutes. It might take 5 to 10 hours or more for the particles to drift down on a site 100 to 200 miles away from the blast.

If no new detonations occur the radiation hazard is probably short-lived. Seven hours after the blast about one tenth of the radiation remains. After two days about one hundredth remains and after two weeks about one thousandth remains. Long term effects of small doses of radiation are still unknown. However there have been survivors of the Hiroshima disaster who lived more than fifty years after the blast.

Radiation sickness is caused by physical and chemical changes in the cells of the body due to radiation from fallout. Large doses of radiation will cause death, while small doses will cause sickness.

Those in good health will recover from the sickness, but the very young and old or those in ill health will experience difficulty. The same dose received over a short period of time is more damaging than if it is received over a longer time period. Radiation sickness is not contagious or infectious. People exposed to fallout radiation do not become radioactive and thereby dangerous to others.

Fallout Shelter In The Home

Cities have fallout shelters and other large buildings to protect citizens from radioactive particles falling from the sky. In the suburbs and rural areas, the basements of homes are probably good enough and with extra care can be made better. Extra protection can be had by adding to a proposed shelter area. Handy materials for lining the shelter are sand, earth, concrete blocks filled with sand, water, books, magazines, and wood. The above materials are listed in order of best protection.

Caught Without A Shelter

If you are outside in the open during a nuclear explosion try to find natural shelter which can be used with the least modification. Do not take more than five minutes to make this decision. Ideal locations are caves, overhanging rocks, deep ditches, or downed logs.

Improve the shelter as you take advantage of its protection. Sweep the ground clean and lie down. Dig a slit trench and stack earth around it. Put a roof over your trench if there are materials available. If the radiation is near, it is better to lie low than to go out gathering roofing materials. Cover yourself with a sheet of plastic, This will keep the fallout off you but it must be shaken often to get the particles away from you.

If the explosion was anticipated then food should have been provided at the shelter site. Canned foods will keep about a year before they should be consumed or replaced. Powdered food, such as milk and cereals last only about six months.

Enough water should have been provided to supply each person with one quart per day. The water in home plumbing would probably be safe to bleed out and use if commercial sources have been cut-off.

Outside water sources may be cloudy or dirty and have to be left to settle or can be strained through paper towels. Boil all water for at least five minutes after the solid particles have been removed. from it. Water can be purified of bacteria by adding twelve drops of iodine per gallon of water.

Radiation passing through food does not contaminate it. Make sure the package is not covered with radioactive fallout before opening it. Fallout particles in lakes will drop to the bottom after a few days and the surface water may be used if the need is urgent. Otherwise give it a few more days.

For disposing human wastes you would want large airtight containers or plastic bags. Remember to provide disinfectant, toilet paper, soap, washcloths, towels, pails, basins, and sanitary napkins. A medicine kit and first aid supplies are essential.

Meat from animals exposed to radiation may be eaten since gamma radiation **will** pass through muscle tissue. However, for safety sake the meat near the bone should be avoided since radiation affects bone material.

III. SURVIVAL IN A REMOTE AREA

In any situation your best move is to let someone know your travel plans, where you are going and when you expect to return and whom to contact if you do not return by the stated time..

Foreword to my book, Short Term Survival Techniques

When faced with a survival problem the biggest enemy is the mind. Don't panic, accept the situation and immediately plan what to do about it. Wherever you may be, remember that humans have lived comfortably in that very spot on the personal resources of the mind, hands, and feet. With these, you too, can survive until you reach a more comfortable situation or someone comes to your rescue.

The framework of this section is based on two assumptions: (1) that you wish to be in the present situation for only a short time period, and (2) you are not being sought by human enemies who wish to kill or capture you. These suggestions will help you to survive, even if pursued, but it does not dwell on escaping pursuit or fighting back.

Remember that you are already a proven survivor. You have survived or escaped many childhood diseases, automobile accidents, epidemics, natural disasters, and the pollution horrors which permeate our environment. All of these have caused the death of someone and they have been a threat to every one of us.

It is in the mind where we decide we wish to survive and once we determine that - we will survive, and our chance for survival increases dramatically.

Many years ago in one of my first survival experiments I had a friend drop me off on a logging road in the Forbes State Forest of southwestern Pennsylvania. The time was early September. He left me on Saturday and was to pick me up on Sunday, eight days later.

My premise was to confine myself to about one square mile of territory which was bounded by a logging road, a three foot wide stream, and a ridge. I took with me the clothes I was wearing, an extra pair of socks, one book of paper matches, a pocket knife, a blanket, and a 9 x 12 foot plastic sheet. Anything I could find in the area could be used in my stay.

Even in this mild exercise there was a lot to learn. I was fortunate to find three tin cans, one large enough to boil food in, even though it was rusted.

One also learns very quickly that there is an absence of toilet paper and appreciates the niceness of soap, a comb, and a toothbrush. .

In that week I was able to kill three birds and two chipmunks with sticks and stones. Other animal food consisted of crayfish, small fish, and salamanders. Plant food included Indian cucumber, dry blackberries, black haws, elderberries, hemlock bark, winter cress, curly dock, and some gnarled apples. Tea was made from red sumac berries, spicebush, goldenrod leaves, and mint. Meat dishes were usually boiled with a bulb of wild onion or a sprig of mint.

In that week I had made a slingshot with the elastic from my underwear waist band, an unsuccessful deadfall to kill chipmunks, a rope from bark and roots, a toothbrush, and a shelter to sleep under. Of the twenty matches in my pack I used seven.

Big problems included bathing, a full day of rain, mosquitoes, and trying to remember what day it was. What if I broke my leg on the second day? What if I broke or lost my knife? Cell phones had not yet been invented.

A person alone in the wilderness had better like his own company for he is very alone with his thoughts. Many people have some trouble with loneliness and boredom. In the wilderness these are magnified. If the days are filled with activity and in anticipation there is no need for boredom. It is a good time to reflect on one's life, one's self, and the future.

If you are going to be alone for a long time then it is good to talk out loud rather than talk to yourself with your inner voice and mind. If you don't talk out loud and you have been out of civilization for quite sometime then you will find it difficult to communicate when you do get back.

One of the best lessons I learned in this exercise was that it takes a large tract of wilderness to support a small group of people. Had I lived in that square mile for any length of time my food supply would have diminished and without cultivation and animal husbandry the situation would be grim. Preparations for winter would have to be well planned and shelter and tools improved.

Large numbers of people could not live off the land for very long without constant migration. In a survival situation where you will have to winter over you must ask yourself the question "How do the animals make it?" If you imitate the animals you will be on the right course.

The previous discussion is about remote areas. Of course, anywhere there are inhabitants you would seek them out if you were not in hostile territory. If ten people were trying to live off the land in, say, Tennessee, they would need to forage in an area of one hundred and fifty square miles. So when one considers survival in arctic or desert conditions, the problem becomes accentuated.

Let me repeat the problems of the mind: (1) no need to panic (2) remember that many people have lived comfortably where you find yourself (3) accept the situation and do something about it (4) combat boredom and loneliness by keeping busy, and (5) make the decision that you want to survive.

SIGNALING SEARCH PLANES

The number of downed planes which are not found by diligent search parties tell us that planes are hard to see from the air and people are even harder. If you have a sending radio you can transmit your approximate position. Of course if you have a GPS system you know exactly where you are. Use the radio only if you suspect aircraft are within its range.

Use smoke by day and flames by night. Add green wood to day fires to create more smoke and add dry wood to night fires to create a bright clean flame. Keep a lot of spare fuel on hand.

Keep signaling aids such as flares and smoke producers dry. Use them only when a rescue party *is* sighted. Signal with mirrors or reflecting devices.

Practice signaling by reflection so you will be prepared when the time comes to actually use it. On hazy days you may not be ale to see a plane but if you are using a reflecting mirror it will be able to see you. Also, signal with a flashlight. .

Climb a large tree and hoist a white flag on top of it by lashing a flag to a pole and tying the pole to the top of the tree.

Mark out S-O-S on the ground with paint, sod, large stones, clothing or some different colored vegetation. Make the letters out of brush in an open area.

Food coloring makes a good attraction when thrown into water. Use it when you see a rescue plane and you are near open water.

STAY PUT OR START MOVING?

Most dramatic survival stories in recent times come from people who are involved in plane crashes. The best advice always seems to be to stay with the aircraft since it will provide you with shelter, fuel, tools, and radio.

The decision to stay in one place or to move is an important one. If you are in a survival situation and hostilities are surrounding you then that is a problem to consider. You would want to make your decision to leave with care. If hostilities exist, where are they in reference to your location?

In U.S. Army lectures we were told if you were down in enemy territory and absolutely had to have help then your best bet is to seek help from an old person.

You could leave the aircraft if you are certain of your position and know you can reach shelter, food, and general help. Even if no organized search parties are looking for you someone in the area may have seen you come down and will come to investigate.

If you have waited several days and no rescue is in sight then the decision to stay or leave must be made. If weather conditions are good there are excellent chances that you will be spotted from the air especially if you came down near a well traveled air route.

If you decide to move on, then try to determine the nearest rescue point from your knowledge of the travel route. Try to estimate your distance from it. Also consider the possibilities of hazards in travel and the supplies needed to reach your destination. What are the physical conditions of your comrades and what is their ability to endure travel? If there are injured persons then send out two of the best fit people to get help. To have one person go for help is dangerous.

If you decide to stay, consider (1) your general health (2) body care (3) camp sanitation (4) program of rest (5) shelter and its improvement (6) water (7) food (8) how long can you hold out.

Consider this if you decide to travel:
(1) which direction (2) what will you take along (3) what will you do before leaving

If you leave the area it might be a good idea to leave some kind of trail in the event a rescue party does get to your plane they will be able to see where you headed.

In a desert environment you would have to be most aware of your water supply and future water supply. In cold arctic areas you would have to have proper equipment and probably the ability to make a fire. In both circumstances it would probably be best to stay with the downed plane.

If you are going to be traveling through desert or arctic landscapes then it might be a good idea to get some knowledge of how people live under those conditions before you set out on the trip. People have been lost and perished in remote areas of Arizona and Alaska. If you follow a stream it will most likely lead you to habitation.

If your plane is down in dense cover then it is best to move to a clearing and set up signal operations. In any area, streams usually lead to civilization or at least settlements. So follow a stream down to its outlet and you will probably find people there who will assist you.

PROVIDING SHELTER

The order of importance of survival options is (1) shelter (2) water (3) food (4) clothing (5) sanitation (6) keeping busy

The kind of shelter you make for yourself and others depends upon your need for protection from insects, rain, cold, or heat. Also your shelter needs depend upon whether or not you will be there for some time or on a temporary basis.

Some general considerations for a shelter site are (1) nearness to fuel and water (2) do not make camp at the base of steep slopes (3) avoid areas of rockfalls, floods, avalanches, and (4) avoid areas where you will be battered by winds.

Do your cooking outside the shelter since

there is danger of carbon monoxide which will make you drowsy and cut into your general efficiency and thought processes. Changes in personal efficiency due to carbon monoxide poisoning are so gradual the victim is not aware of them.

Studies of people caught in traffic jams have indicated a loss of mental alertness from breathing in exhaust fumes. This intake of excess carbon monoxide is believed to be the cause of most fender bender accidents in rush hour traffic. So, breathing in carbon monoxide in a make shift camp would be hazardous to your efficiency.

Avoid sleeping on the bare ground since ground dampness will make you very uncomfortable. In most areas you can make a bed of grass or soft brush or evergreen boughs. Pick a bed site on level well-drained ground, free from rocks and roots. If you have to sleep on bare ground then dig a small depression for your hips and shoulders and try it out before you set your shelter or bed down for the night.

When using cloth or plastic for a shelter the ends must be tied down in order for the shelter to remain where you want it.

FIRE MAKING

You will need fire for warmth, for keeping dry, for signaling, for cooking, and for purifying water. Don't build a fire too big. Small fires require less fuel and are easier to control. Heat from a small fire is easily concentrated. Small fires arranged in a circle around you are more effective in keeping you warm than one large fire.

Prepare the location of your fire with care. Clear away leaves, twigs, dry grass, and moss. If the ground is dry, scrape down to the bare dirt. If the fire must be built on snow or ice or wet ground then build it on a platform of logs or flat stones. In swamp areas you can build a small platform among trees, get out of the water and even build a small fire on your platform.

Build the fire against a rock wall or a wall of logs which will serve as a reflector and prevent the wind from whipping it about. A cooking fire should be walled in by logs or stones to concentrate heat and to form a platform for your pot.

The three types of burnable material needed for a fire are tinder, kindling, and fuel. Tinder is a fine dry material which takes a spark to a flame easily or can be easily started with a match. Kindling is small dry fuel which will take the flame from tinder and make it hot enough to burn heavier fuel logs or wood.

Both the tinder and kindling must be easily set aflame. If you have matches, tinder may be fine dry twigs or fine wood shavings. If you have a knife then make some fine wood shavings. Natural kindling woods are thin sticks,dry thin wood, dry bark, wood shavings, palm leaves, dry ferns, dry straw or grass. Split sticks to be used as kindling. Store kindling to keep it dry. Cardboard boxes and paper are of course good kindling material. Gasoline poured on the kindling and fuel give it an extra burning start. Don't pour much on it and NEVER pour gasoline on a fire that *is* already started or smoldering.

For fuel, use dry standing dead wood and dry dead branches. It *is* best to get these directly from an upright dead tree. If you have no tools then pound the dead wood on a hard surface to break it. The inside of large dead branches would be dry even if the outside was wet. Green wood will burn if it is finely split. Use rocks as wedges to split large pieces of wood.

In treeless areas look for dry grass or dry animal,dung. Use animal fat or oil of any kind, and a mixture of gasoline and practically anything else.

In cold weather stuff your sleeves, pant legs, and waist area with dry dead leaves, dry moss, or dry grass.

STARTING A FIRE

Get all your materials together before you try to start the fire. Make certain that your matches, tinder, and kindling are dry. Have enough fuel on hand to keep your fire going.

Arrange your kindling in a small pyramid close enough together to transfer the flame from one piece to the other. Leave a small opening for lighting. If you have a candle light it with the match. This will save your matches if you have difficulty with the light. If you have no candle, make a shave stick or use a bundle of dry twigs tied loosely. Shield your match from the wind. Apply your lighted candle or twigs to the windward side of the pile.

Once the kindling is burning then lay on small pieces of larger fuel. Add larger material as the fire takes hold. Don't let your fire smother by loading it down with heavy materials. Don't waste fuel by making a fire too big. Allow open spaces on the sides and underneath for air draft.

MAINTAINING HEALTH

Keeping in good health is especially important when you are alone and on your own. Here are some general rules for keeping healthy.

Drink enough safe water to avoid dehydration. If water is scarce or if difficult to get then avoid exertion which may cause sweating. Save your strength. Get enough sleep and avoid fatigue. Even if you can't sleep it is best to lie down for a long period of time to loosen up and relax. Stop worrying; it is a useless activity.

If you are working hard or walking then make it a firm policy to rest for ten minutes in each hour.

If your feet hurt, stop and take care of them for it will save you trouble later on. Examine your feet when you stop, to see if there are any blisters developing. If so, cover that area with tape if you have some. If you have a blister do not break it since this will encourage infection. If it does break, leave the loose skin on it and apply a dressing.

Your skin is the first line of defense against body infection. Use an antiseptic on even the smallest scratch. Keep your fingernails short to prevent infection. Keep from scratching. In warm climates, a small infection can turn bad in a short time.

Intestinal upsets and diarrhea can be caused by a change of water and food. It can also be dangerous to your intestines when you are extremely tired or working in hot weather or over-eating. Dirty dishes and hands are a prime source of diarrhea. In strange territory, purify all water before drinking or cooking in it. A minute of boiling will purify most water. Make it at least five minutes to be certain it is purified.

If possible, always wash your hands with soap and water before handling food. If a member of your group gets diarrhea take care to enforce measures for proper disposal of human waste. Insure cleanliness in handling food and water. A minute of precaution is worth preventing two days of illness.

To treat diarrhea it is best to rest and not eat solid foods for a full day. Take in only liquids, soup, or tea made from local herbs. Commercial coffee and tea have caffeine which sometimes will irritate an already irritated digestive system. Just drinking warm water is relaxing to both mind and bowel.

Keep drinking lots of water if it is available. Take some salt to replace that which has been lost. As one recovers from diarrhea it is best to eat small meals often instead of a large meal once.

Don't worry about bowel movements since they will not be as frequent in a survival situation.

Keep your body and clothing clean. You will feel better and keep free from skin infections and parasites. Examine each other for external parasites.

Keep your camp area clean. Dump your trash and garbage in a pit or a spot far away from your camp. Dig a latrine or a slit trench and cover up your human waste as soon as you create it. Keep the latrine away from your water supply.

Keep Your Head

There may be   some situations we cannot avoid
where we might find ourselves in danger. But, if we
are mentally prepared for such a possible event we
will survive. As Rudyard Kipling said in one of his
poems, "If you can keep your head while others all
about you are losing theirs and blaming it on you,
you'll be a man my son." In your case, "you'll be a
survivor."

The previous Kipling lines also apply to the advice
and reflections presented at the beginning of this
work.

Internet Identity Theft ?

We all get a lot of messages on our email accounts.
Some may be scams. How can you protect yourself
from downloading the scams?   I once downloaded an
enticing piece of literature and after it came up an
official looking notice from the FBI said I had
violated some law such as KF 13245. My computer
froze. There were explicit directions on how to
unfreeze my computer. This procedure involved
going to a commercial outlet and obtaining a $300
credit card and swiping it off to some location.
Fortunately, my son was home at the time and he
reset my computer to the day before I had become
involved in the situation. He said the FBI was aware
of such scams and have made many arrests connected
with them.

Some basic maneuvers:
Don't click on the links, especially links that promise something sensational, shocking, or exclusive such as photos or videos.

A Friend, might not be anyone you know. Scammers hack social media accounts and will send fake links to the victim's online friends. If you have any doubts, don't click on the link. Even if it was sent by a friend, there is nothing that critical for you to take a chance.

Delete unsolicited emails and social media messages if you don't know who sent them. If any message creates a doubt in your mind, don't open it.

Hover: Move your cursor over the link and it will tell you something about it. If you don't recognize the website don't click on it.

Sometimes scammers will place fake links on Facebook that will give them your account if you participate. They then sell these accounts,   If you run across these fake links on your social pagea report them to Twitter or Facebook.

A Word on Some Relationships · Your emotional survival.

There are people in our society who do not deny themselves anything material, financial and emotional. Usually these people cannot acquire these commodities by their own efforts. They go into debt or get themselves into romantic or social situations that often make life uncomfortable to themselves and to those associated with them. Usually these are family members since that association carries with it a sense of obligation as well as a sense of guilt.

These are people who seem to have a bottomless pit of need. They look about to see who will assist them in their endeavors. Once they find someone to assist them they no longer need to discipline and extricate themselves from the bad situation because they now can continue in that habit of living in emotional and financial debt. Now, they are abetted by their victim.

No one can make you a victim without your cooperation. Somehow you must find the courage to stop cooperating with their habits. Few of us have that courage, since the situation has moved from charity to obligation. We then continue to lose our own peace of mind and fret about the safety and well being of those who have imposed upon us. We lose sleep, while they sleep soundly. We have a feeling of obligation connected with some sort of guilt.

The solution
When you have done all you can for someone, let them be. Let them do whatever they want. Do not stay involved in that level of the relationship.

Some people are immune to good advice.
Accept that and move on.